Your Guide to Smart Living:

Creating a Cost-Effective

and Efficient Smart Home

Chapter 1: Introduction to Smart Homes

In this chapter, we will discuss what a smart home is and how it can

benefit you. We will explore the different devices and technologies that

are commonly used in a smart home and how they can make your life

easier.

Chapter 2: Choosing the Right Smart Devices

In this chapter, we will discuss the various types of smart devices that

are available on the market and how to choose the right ones for your

home. We will also explore the different features and functions of these

devices and how they can help you save money and improve your

quality of life.

Chapter 3: Setting Up Your Smart Home

In this chapter, we will walk you through the process of setting up your

smart home. We will discuss the different steps involved in this

process, such as connecting your devices to the internet, setting up

your smart hub, and configuring your devices.

Chapter 4: Creating Smart Routines

In this chapter, we will discuss how to create smart routines that can

help you save time and money. We will explore the different ways in which you can automate your home, such as setting up automatic

lighting and temperature control, and scheduling your appliances to

turn on and off at specific times.

Chapter 5: Smart Home Security

In this chapter, we will discuss the importance of smart home security

and how to keep your home safe from hackers and other cyber threats.

We will explore the different security features that are available in smart home devices and how to use them to protect your home and

your personal information.

Chapter 6: Smart Home Energy Efficiency

In this chapter, we will discuss how to make your smart home more

energy-efficient. We will explore the different ways in which you can

save energy and money, such as using smart thermostats, smart

lighting, and energy-efficient appliances.

Chapter 7: Troubleshooting Your Smart Home

In this chapter, we will discuss common issues that you may encounter when setting up and using your smart home. We will explore different troubleshooting methods and provide tips on how to resolve these issues quickly and effectively.

Chapter 8: Future of Smart Homes

In this final chapter, we will discuss the future of smart homes and how

they will continue to evolve and improve over time. We will explore new

technologies and devices that are currently in development and how

they will impact the way we live and interact with our homes.

Preface

In recent years, my home has evolved from a mere space filled with modern conveniences to a sanctuary of efficiency and cleanliness, thanks to smart appliances and accessories. Our transition to a smart home has not only enhanced our hygiene but also significantly improved our health. If you share my passion for controlling your home with just a touch of a button, automating daily tasks, and enjoying a life of comfort and efficiency, then this guide is for you. Note that prices may change since the publication of this book.

Why A Smart Home?

Many people often perceive smart homes and their components as

luxurious or even extravagant. However, manufacturers and I view it

differently. Transforming your home into a smart living space

doesn't necessarily mean breaking the bank; it can actually be an investment that pays off in the long run. Here are a few reasons why

it's smart to go smart:

Savings:

Turning your home into a smart home can result in substantial

savings on electricity, water, and other utility bills. For instance, you

can schedule smart lights to turn off automatically when you're not

home. This can be achieved by linking your smart lighting system to a digital assistant like Google Home or Alexa, creating a "leaving home" routine that switches off all lights when activated. Best of all, these assistant apps are free to download on iOS and Android.

Efficiency:

Imagine waking up to a personalized news update read to you by a virtual assistant. This isn't just about text-to-speech functionality; I'm talking about an AI assistant that can tailor the information to your preferences. Automated systems can also replace or reduce the

need for full-time helpers, freeing up your time and resources.

Chapter 1: Introduction to Smart Homes

Smart homes have transitioned from being a novelty to a modern standard for those aiming to streamline their lives and enhance their homes. A smart home is equipped with interconnected devices that can be remotely managed via a central hub, such as a smartphone

or voice-controlled devices like Amazon Echo or Google Home.

Benefits of a Smart Home

Smart homes offer a plethora of advantages including time, money,

and energy savings, along with an elevated quality of life. Whether

it's automating the adjustment of your thermostat or the monitoring of your home security, smart homes provide both convenience and

peace of mind.

Common Smart Devices

From smart thermostats that adjust your home's temperature to

smart security systems that alert you to suspicious activity, there's

an array of smart devices designed to make your life more

convenient, efficient, and secure.

1. Smart Thermostats

Automatically adjust temperatures according to your preferences and daily patterns, resulting in energy and cost savings.

2. Smart Lighting

With smart lighting, you can control the lighting in your home remotely, set up schedules to turn lights on and off automatically, and even adjust the brightness or color of the light.

3. Smart Security Systems

These devices include smart locks, doorbells, and cameras that allow you to monitor your home's security remotely and receive alerts if any suspicious activity is detected.

4. Smart Appliances

Smart appliances such as refrigerators, ovens, and washing machines can make your daily routine more convenient and efficient. These devices can be controlled remotely and can alert you when they need maintenance.

5. Voice-Controlled Devices

Voice-controlled devices such as Amazon Echo or Google Home allow you to control your smart devices using your voice, making it easier to complete tasks hands-free.

6. Smart Plugs

These devices allow you to make your non-smart devices smart

by controlling their power remotely. You can set schedules to

turn devices on and off automatically or control them using

your smartphone.

7. **Smart Speakers**

Smart speakers such as Amazon Echo or Google Home allow you to control your smart devices using voice commands. They also allow you to listen to music, news, and weather reports.

8. Smart Smoke Detectors

These devices are an essential safety device for any home.

They can detect smoke and alert you to a fire emergency, even if you're not at home.

9. Smart Water Monitors

These devices can help you save money on your water bills by

detecting leaks and monitoring your water usage. Some models

can send alerts to your phone if they detect a leak, allowing you

to take action quickly and prevent costly water damage.

10. Smart Cameras

Smart cameras allow you to monitor your home remotely and can send alerts to your phone if any suspicious activity is detected. Some models also come with two-way audio, allowing you to communicate with people in your home.

11. Smart Door Locks

These devices allow you to lock and unlock your doors remotely using your smartphone or voice-controlled device.

Some models can also send alerts to your phone if anyone tries

to tamper with the lock.

12. Smart Blinds and Shades

Smart blinds and shades can be controlled remotely, allowing

you to adjust the lighting and privacy of your home. They can be

controlled using your smartphone, voice-controlled device, or

set up on a schedule to adjust automatically.

13. Smart Sprinklers

Smart sprinklers can help you save money on your water bills by adjusting your watering schedule based on the weather and soil moisture levels. They can be controlled remotely using your smartphone, and some models can even detect leaks in your irrigation system.

14. Smart Vacuum Cleaners

Smart vacuum cleaners can save you time and energy by

cleaning your home automatically. They can be programmed to

clean specific areas of your home, and some models even use

artificial intelligence to map out the layout of your home and

clean more efficiently.

By incorporating the right devices tailored to your needs, you can build a smart home that not only simplifies your life but also provides a layer of security and cost-efficiency. In the chapters that follow, we will delve deeper into how to select, set up, and integrate these smart devices for a seamless smart home experience.

Chapter 2: Choosing the Right Smart Devices

Choosing the right smart devices for your home can be overwhelming with the multitude of options available in the market. In this chapter, we will guide you through the process of selecting the right smart devices that meet your needs and fit your budget.

Step 1: Determine Your Needs

Before purchasing any smart device, it is important to assess your needs. Identify the areas in your home that require automation and where a smart device could save you time, money, or improve your quality of life. For instance, if you want to save energy bills, a smart thermostat may be the right choice. If you're looking for convenience, a smart speaker or voice-controlled device may be the ideal option.

Step 2: Consider Compatibility

When choosing smart devices, ensure that they are compatible with

each other and with your chosen smart hub. Most smart hubs work

with multiple devices, but it is important to confirm that the device you

want to buy is compatible. For instance, if you want to use Amazon

Alexa as your smart hub, ensure that the smart devices you want to

purchase are compatible with Alexa.

Step 3: Research Brands and Models

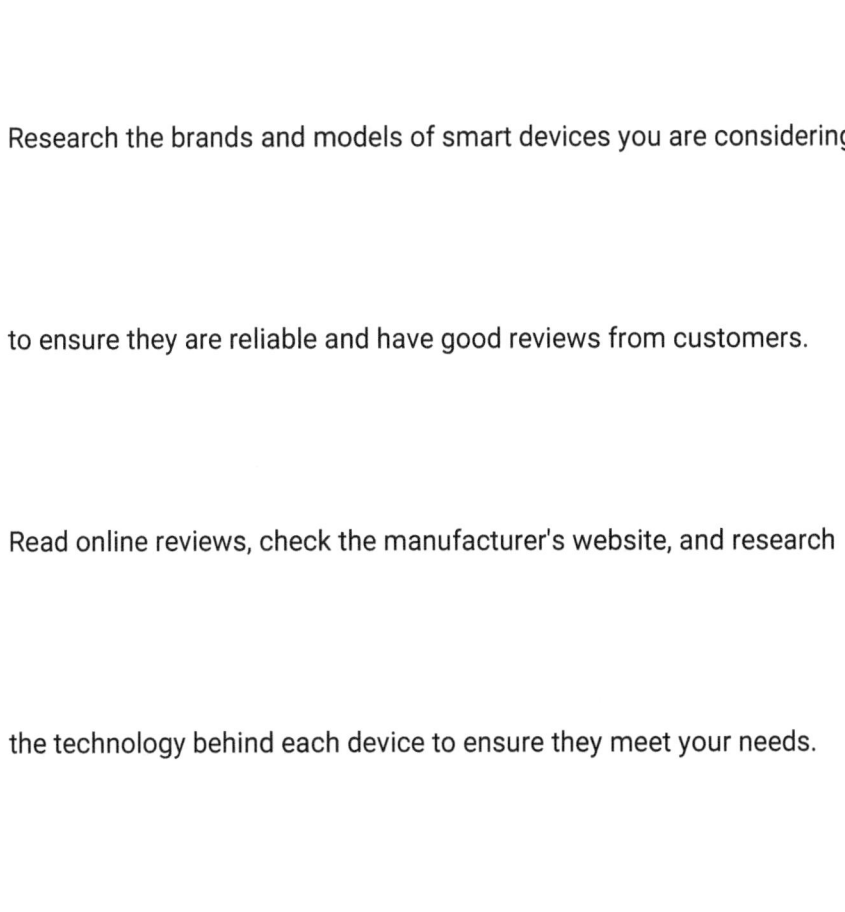

Research the brands and models of smart devices you are considering

to ensure they are reliable and have good reviews from customers.

Read online reviews, check the manufacturer's website, and research

the technology behind each device to ensure they meet your needs.

Step 4: Consider Features and Functions

Consider the features and functions of each smart device. For instance, a smart thermostat may include features like occupancy sensing, auto-learning, and scheduling. A smart lock may come with features like auto-locking, guest access, and remote access. Consider the features and functions that matter most to you.

Step 5: Budget

Smart devices come with varying price points. Consider your budget and how much you are willing to spend on each device. While some smart devices may seem expensive, they could save you money in the long run on energy bills or repair costs.

Some of the popular smart devices include smart thermostats, smart lighting, smart security systems, smart appliances, and voice-controlled devices. By following the above steps, you can choose the right smart devices for your home that meet your needs and fit your budget. In the

next chapter, we will discuss how to set up your smart home and get

your devices working together.

Step 6: Consider Interoperability

Interoperability refers to how well smart devices work with other devices and systems. A device that is interoperable can communicate with other devices and systems in your home, even if they are from different brands. This can be important if you plan to expand your smart home in the future or want to integrate your smart home with other systems like home automation or security.

Step 7: Check Data Privacy and Security

When choosing smart devices, it is important to consider the security and privacy of your data. Smart devices collect data on your behaviors and usage patterns, and this data can be vulnerable to hacking and data breaches. Choose devices from reputable brands that prioritize data privacy and security.

Step 8: Check Customer Support and Warranty

When purchasing smart devices, check the warranty and customer support provided by the manufacturer. Ensure that you can get help if you encounter any issues or defects in the device. A good warranty and customer support can save you money in the long run.

By following these steps, you can choose the right smart devices for your home and ensure that they work well together. In the next chapter, we will explore how to set up your smart home and get your devices working together seamlessly.

Step 9: Assess User-Friendliness

When selecting smart devices, consider their ease of use. Some devices may have a steep learning curve or require advanced technical knowledge to set up and operate. Look for devices that have an intuitive interface and easy-to-follow instructions for installation and

use.

Step 10: Consider Energy Efficiency

Energy efficiency is an important consideration when choosing smart

devices. Look for devices that are energy-efficient and can help you

save money on energy bills. Smart thermostats, smart lighting, and smart appliances are some of the devices that can help you save

energy and reduce your carbon footprint.

Step 11: Think About Aesthetics

Smart devices are not just functional but can also be stylish and

aesthetically pleasing. Consider the design and style of the device, and

how it will fit in with your home's décor. Many smart devices are designed to be sleek and minimalistic, but there are also options for

more decorative devices that blend in with your home's style.

By considering these additional factors, you can choose smart devices

that not only meet your functional needs but also fit with your lifestyle,

aesthetic preferences, and environmental goals. With the right smart

devices in your home, you can enjoy convenience, cost savings, and

improved quality of life.

Chapter 3: Setting Up Your Smart Home

In this chapter, we will guide you through the process of setting up your smart home. We will discuss the steps involved in connecting your devices to the internet, setting up your smart hub, and configuring your

devices for optimal performance.

Step 1: Choose Your Smart Hub

A smart hub is the central device that connects and controls all of your

smart devices. There are many different smart hubs available, ranging

from voice-controlled devices like Amazon Echo and Google Home to

dedicated smart home controllers like Samsung SmartThings and

Apple HomeKit. Choose a smart hub that is compatible with the devices you want to use and fits within your budget.

Step 2: Connect Your Smart Devices

Once you have chosen your smart hub, it's time to connect your smart devices. Most smart devices are connected to the internet using Wi-Fi or Bluetooth, and they can be connected to your smart hub using a companion app or by scanning a QR code. Follow the instructions

provided by the manufacturer to connect your devices to the hub.

Step 3: Create Smart Routines

Smart routines are pre-set actions that your smart home can perform

based on specific triggers or schedules. For instance, you could set up

a routine that turns on your lights and adjusts the temperature when

you arrive home or a routine that turns off all of your devices at night.

Setting up smart routines can help you save time and energy and make

your home more convenient.

Step 4: Configure Your Smart Home Settings

Once your devices are connected and your routines are set up, it's time

to configure your smart home settings. You can adjust settings like the

temperature of your smart thermostat, the brightness of your smart lighting, or the sensitivity of your smart security system. Fine-tuning your settings can help optimize your smart home's performance.

Step 5: Troubleshoot Any Issues

If you encounter any issues with your smart home, don't panic. Most issues can be resolved with a quick troubleshooting session. Check your device's manual or the manufacturer's website for guidance on common issues and solutions. If you can't resolve the issue, contact

the manufacturer's customer support for assistance.

By following these steps, you can set up your smart home and get your

devices working together seamlessly. In the next chapter, we will

explore how to create smart routines and automate your home for

maximum convenience and energy efficiency.

Step 6: Secure Your Smart Home

Smart home security is crucial to protect your home and personal information from cyber threats. When setting up your smart home, take the necessary steps to secure your devices and network. Change default passwords, enable two-factor authentication, and keep your firmware and software up to date. Consider investing in a reputable antivirus software and a VPN to secure your internet connection.

Step 7: Customize Your Smart Home

One of the benefits of a smart home is the ability to customize it to fit your needs and preferences. You can adjust your smart routines, create new ones, and add new devices to your smart home system.

Experiment with different settings and devices to find the perfect combination that works for you.

Step 8: Explore New Smart Home Devices

As technology advances, new smart home devices and features are constantly being developed. Keep an eye out for new devices that can improve your smart home experience and help you save even more time and energy. Stay informed by reading reviews, subscribing to tech newsletters, and following technology blogs.

Step 9: Consider Professional Installation

If you are not confident in your ability to set up your smart home, consider hiring a professional installer. Many smart home manufacturers offer installation services, and there are also third-party installers who can help you set up your devices and ensure they work properly.

By considering these additional steps, you can set up a secure, customized, and optimized smart home that meets your needs and fits your lifestyle. With the right smart home system in place, you can enjoy maximum convenience, energy efficiency, and security.

Step 10: Monitor Your Smart Home

Regular monitoring of your smart home can help you identify issues before they become major problems. Use your smart home app or hub to check the status of your devices and monitor your energy usage. You can also set up alerts to notify you if a device is not working correctly or if a security breach is detected.

Step 11: Upgrade Your Smart Home

As your smart home system becomes older, it may become outdated or less efficient. Consider upgrading your smart devices and hub periodically to take advantage of new features and improved performance. Upgrading can help you save money on energy bills,

improve your home's security, and add new features to your smart

home.

Step 12: Share Your Smart Home Experience

Share your smart home experience with others to help them discover

the benefits of a smart home. You can share your experience on social

media, write a review of your devices, or simply talk to friends and family about your smart home system. Sharing your experience can

help others make informed decisions about their own smart home

setups.

By following these additional steps, you can ensure that your smart

home remains secure, up-to-date, and optimized for maximum

convenience and energy efficiency. With regular monitoring and upgrades, you can continue to enjoy the benefits of a smart home for

years to come.

Chapter 4: Creating Smart Routines

In this chapter, we will explore how to create smart routines

that can help you save time and money. We will discuss the

different ways in which you can automate your home, such as

setting up automatic lighting and temperature control, and

scheduling your appliances to turn on and off at specific

times.

Step 1: Identify Your Routine Needs

The first step in creating a smart routine is to identify your

routine needs. Consider your daily routine and think about

tasks that you could automate to save time and energy. For

instance, you could create a routine that turns off all of your lights when you leave for work or a routine that turns on your

coffee maker when you wake up.

Step 2: Choose Your Smart Home Devices

Once you have identified your routine needs, choose the smart

devices that can help you automate those tasks. For example,

you could use smart plugs to turn on and off your appliances, or a smart thermostat to adjust the temperature in your home.

Make sure the devices you choose are compatible with your smart home hub and each other.

Step 3: Set Up Your Smart Routines

Now that you have your smart devices in place, it's time to set up your smart routines. You can use your smart home app or hub to set up routines based on specific triggers, such as time of day, location, or sensor activity. For instance, you could create a routine that turns off all of your lights when you leave home or a routine that turns on your porch light when motion is detected.

Step 4: Customize Your Smart Routines

Customizing your smart routines can help you optimize your smart home experience. For example, you could adjust the brightness of your lights or the temperature settings of your smart thermostat to fit your preferences. You can also adjust the timing of your routines to fit your schedule.

Step 5: Test and Refine Your Smart Routines

After setting up your smart routines, test them to ensure they work properly. Monitor the performance of your routines and make adjustments as needed to optimize their efficiency.

Refining your routines can help you save even more time and energy.

By following these steps, you can create smart routines that help you save time, money, and energy. In the next chapter, we will discuss smart home security and how to keep your home safe from cyber threats.

Step 6: Expand Your Smart Routines

Once you have established your smart routines, consider expanding

them to include more tasks and devices. You can add new smart

devices to your system or create new routines to automate additional

tasks. Expanding your smart routines can help you save even more

time and energy.

Step 7: Take Advantage of Voice Control

Many smart home devices are voice-controlled, allowing you to control them with simple voice commands. Take advantage of voice control to make your smart home even more convenient. For example, you can use voice commands to turn on and off your lights or adjust the temperature in your **home.**

Step 8: Create Smart Routines for Energy

Efficiency

Smart routines can help you save energy and reduce your carbon footprint. For example, you can set up a routine that turns off all of your devices when you leave the house or a routine that adjusts your thermostat settings to save energy when you're not home. Creating smart routines for energy efficiency can help you save money on your energy bills and reduce your environmental impact.

Step 9: Use Geofencing for Automatic Triggers

Geofencing is a feature that uses GPS technology to trigger smart home routines based on your location. For example, you can set up a routine that turns on your lights and adjusts the temperature in your home when you're a certain distance from your house. Geofencing can help you automate your routines even further and make your smart

home even more convenient.

By following these additional steps, you can create smart routines that

are customized, efficient, and convenient. With voice control,

geofencing, and routines for energy efficiency, you can take advantage

of all the benefits of a smart home and make your life even easier.

Chapter 5: Smart Home Security

In this chapter, we will discuss the importance of smart home security

and how to keep your home safe from hackers and other cyber threats.

We will explore the different security features that are available in smart home devices and how to use them to protect your home and

your personal information.

Step 1: Secure Your Network

We The first step in securing your smart home is to secure your

network. Use a strong password for your Wi-Fi network and enable

WPA2 encryption. You can also hide your network name and set up a

guest network to keep your devices separate from your guests' devices.

Step 2: Choose Secure Smart Home Devices

Choose smart home devices that have strong security features, such as encryption, automatic software updates, and two-factor authentication. Research the devices you plan to buy and look for any security vulnerabilities or known security issues.

Step 3: Keep Your Devices Up to Date

Keeping your devices up to date with the latest firmware and software updates is critical for security. Many smart home devices offer automatic updates, but you should also check for updates regularly to ensure that your devices are secure.

Step 4: Enable Two-Factor Authentication

Two-factor authentication adds an extra layer of security to your smart home devices. This requires a second form of identification, such as a text message or fingerprint, in addition to your password to access your device. Enable two-factor authentication whenever possible to keep your devices secure.

Step 5: Use Strong Passwords

Use strong, unique passwords for your smart home devices and change them regularly. Avoid using the same password for multiple devices and use a password manager to keep track of your passwords.

Step 6: Monitor Your Devices

Regularly monitor your smart home devices for any suspicious activity, such as unauthorized access or unusual network activity. Use your smart home app or hub to check the status of your devices and set up alerts to notify you if any suspicious activity is detected.

By following these steps, you can ensure that your smart home is secure and protected from cyber threats. In the next chapter, we will discuss how to make your smart home more energy-efficient.

Step 7: Disable Remote Access for Unused Devices

If you have smart devices that you no longer use or need, disable remote access for those devices. This can prevent unauthorized access and reduce your risk of a cyber attack.

Step 8: Set Up a Firewall

Set up a firewall on your router to protect your smart home devices from external threats. A firewall can help prevent hackers from accessing your smart home devices and stealing your personal information.

Step 9: Be Cautious with Third-Party Integrations

Be cautious when integrating third-party devices or services with your smart home system. Research the third-party device or service and make sure it has strong security features and a good reputation.

Step 10: Review Privacy Policies

Review the privacy policies of your smart home devices and ensure that they are transparent about their data collection and use practices. Be cautious of devices or services that collect unnecessary personal information or sell your data to third-party advertisers.

Step 11: Educate Yourself and Your Family

Educate yourself and your family about smart home security and best practices for staying safe online. Make sure everyone knows how to use strong passwords, enable two-factor authentication, and recognize phishing scams and other cyber threats.

By following these additional steps, you can improve the security of

your smart home and protect your personal information from cyber

threats. With a secure smart home, you can enjoy all the benefits of a

connected and convenient home without compromising on privacy and

security.

Chapter 6: Smart Home

Energy Efficiency

In this chapter, we will discuss how to make your smart home more

energy-efficient. We will explore the different ways in which you can save energy and money, such as using smart thermostats, smart

lighting, and energy-efficient appliances.

Step 1: Use Smart Thermostats

Smart thermostats can help you save energy and money by

automatically adjusting the temperature in your home based on your

schedule and preferences. They can learn your habits and adjust the temperature accordingly, reducing your energy consumption and

lowering your utility bills.

Step 2: Install Energy-Efficient Lighting

Replacing your traditional light bulbs with energy-efficient LEDs can

help you save energy and money. Smart lighting can also help you save

energy by allowing you to control your lights remotely and set

schedules for turning them on and off.

Step 3: Use Energy-Efficient Appliances

Using energy-efficient appliances can help you save energy and money over time. Look for appliances with the ENERGY STAR label, which indicates that they meet energy efficiency guidelines set by the U.S. Environmental Protection Agency.

Step 4: Monitor Your Energy Usage

Monitoring your energy usage can help you identify areas where you can save energy and money. Use your smart home app or hub to monitor your energy usage and identify any devices or appliances that are using too much energy.

Step 5: Set Up Smart Home Routines for Energy Efficiency

Setting up smart home routines for energy efficiency can help you save

energy and money automatically. For example, you can set up a routine

that turns off all of your devices when you leave the house or a routine

that adjusts your thermostat settings to save energy when you're not

home.

Step 6: Use Solar Energy

Using solar energy can help you reduce your dependence on traditional energy sources and save money on your energy bills. You can install solar panels on your roof or use portable solar panels to generate your own energy.

By following these steps, you can make your smart home more energy-efficient and save money on your energy bills. With smart thermostats, energy-efficient lighting, and appliances, and energy monitoring, you can take control of your energy usage and reduce your environmental

impact.

Step 7: Consider Energy Storage

Energy storage systems can help you store excess energy generated by

your solar panels or other renewable energy sources. This stored

energy can be used during peak hours or when there is a power outage, reducing your reliance on the grid and saving you money on your

energy bills.

Step 8: Use Smart Power Strips

Smart power strips can help you save energy by automatically turning

off devices that are not in use. They can also monitor your energy

usage and provide insights into which devices are using the most

energy.

Step 9: Choose Energy-Efficient Windows and

Insulation

Choosing energy-efficient windows and insulation can help you reduce

your energy consumption and lower your utility bills. Energy-efficient

windows can help regulate the temperature in your home, reducing the

need for heating and cooling.

Step 10: Use Smart Irrigation Systems

If you have a garden or lawn, using a smart irrigation system can help you save water and reduce your water bills. These systems can automatically adjust the watering schedule based on weather conditions, soil moisture, and other factors.

Step 11: Monitor Your Carbon Footprint

Monitoring your carbon footprint can help you track your progress in

reducing your environmental impact. Use a carbon footprint calculator

to calculate your carbon footprint and identify areas where you can

make improvements.

By following these additional steps, you can make your smart home

even more energy-efficient and reduce your environmental impact. With

energy storage, smart power strips, energy-efficient windows, and smart irrigation systems, you can take control of your energy usage and

make a positive impact on the planet.

Chapter 7: Troubleshooting

Your Smart Home

In this chapter, we will discuss common issues that you may encounter when setting up and using your smart home. We will explore different troubleshooting methods and provide tips on how to resolve these

issues quickly and effectively.

Step 1: Check Your Network Connection

If your smart home devices are not responding or connecting to your

network, the first step is to check your network connection. Make sure

that your Wi-Fi network is working properly and that your devices are

within range of your router.

Step 2: Restart Your Devices

Restarting your devices can often resolve common issues, such as connectivity problems or software glitches. Try unplugging your devices from the power source and plugging them back in after a few minutes.

Step 3: Update Firmware and Software

Updating your device's firmware and software can help fix bugs and

improve performance. Check for updates regularly and install them as

soon as they become available.

Step 4: Reset Your Devices

If all else fails, you may need to reset your devices to their factory

settings. This will erase all settings and data on the device and restore

it to its original state.

Step 5: Contact Customer Support

If you are still having issues with your smart home devices, contact customer support for assistance. Many manufacturers offer customer support services to help you troubleshoot issues and resolve problems quickly.

Step 6: Keep Your Devices Clean

Dirt and dust can accumulate on your smart home devices and interfere with their performance. Keep your devices clean by wiping them down regularly with a soft cloth.

Step 7: Check for Interference

Other devices or appliances in your home may be interfering with your smart home devices. Try moving your devices to a different location or turning off other devices to see if that resolves the issue.

By following these steps, you can troubleshoot common issues with

your smart home devices and ensure that they are working properly.

With a little patience and persistence, you can quickly resolve any

issues and get back to enjoying your smart home.

Step 8: Check Device Compatibility

Some smart home devices may not be compatible with your existing

smart home system or with other devices in your home. Check the compatibility of your devices before purchasing them to ensure that

they will work together.

Step 9: Review User Manuals and Online Resources

User manuals and online resources can provide valuable information

on troubleshooting issues with your smart home devices. Review these resources to learn more about your devices and how to resolve

common issues.

Step 10: Use the Right Power Source

Using the right power source for your smart home devices is important

for ensuring that they work properly. Make sure that you are using the

correct voltage and amperage for your devices, and avoid using

adapters or power strips that are not designed for your devices.

Step 11: Protect Your Devices from Physical Damage

Physical damage to your smart home devices can interfere with their performance and cause issues. Protect your devices from damage by placing them in a safe location and avoiding dropping or mishandling them.

Step 12: Monitor Your Devices Regularly

Monitoring your smart home devices regularly can help you identify issues before they become major problems. Use your smart home app or hub to monitor the performance of your devices and look for any unusual behavior or patterns.

By following these additional steps, you can troubleshoot issues with your smart home devices and keep them working properly. With a little effort and attention, you can ensure that your smart home is running

smoothly and providing you with all the benefits of a connected and

convenient living space.

Chapter 8: Future of Smart Homes

In this final chapter, we will discuss the future of smart homes and how

they will continue to evolve and improve over time. We will explore new technologies and devices that are currently in development and how they will impact the way we live and interact with our homes.

Step 1: Integration of Artificial Intelligence

Artificial intelligence (AI) is poised to revolutionize the way we interact with our smart homes. With AI-powered voice assistants and other devices, our homes will become even more intuitive and personalized, responding to our needs and preferences in real-time.

Step 2: Smart Homes and Health

Smart homes will also play an increasingly important role in promoting health and wellness. With sensors and wearables that can track vital signs and other health data, our homes will become a hub for personalized health monitoring and care.

Step 3: Increased Connectivity

As more devices and appliances become connected to the internet, our smart homes will become even more interconnected and responsive.

This will create new opportunities for automation and optimization, as well as new challenges in managing and securing these interconnected systems.

Step 4: Expansion of Smart Home Ecosystems

Smart home ecosystems will continue to expand, with more devices and services being integrated into existing systems. This will create new opportunities for innovation and collaboration, as well as new challenges in managing and coordinating these complex ecosystems.

Step 5: Privacy and Security

As smart homes become more interconnected and reliant on data, privacy and security will become even more important. Smart home users will need to be vigilant in protecting their personal information

and securing their devices from hackers and other cyber threats.

Step 6: Environmental Sustainability

Smart homes will also play an important role in promoting

environmental sustainability. With energy-efficient devices, renewable

energy sources, and smart monitoring systems, our homes will become

a key component in the fight against climate change.

By following these developments in the future of smart homes, we can

prepare ourselves for the exciting possibilities and challenges that lie

ahead. As we continue to push the boundaries of what is possible, our

smart homes will become an increasingly integral part of our lives,

providing us with comfort, convenience, and security for years to come.

Step 7: Augmented Reality and Virtual Reality

Augmented reality (AR) and virtual reality (VR) are also expected to play a role in the future of smart homes. AR and VR technology can be used to create immersive experiences in the home, such as virtual home tours, interactive home design, and virtual home assistants.

Step 8: Smart Home Standards and Interoperability

Smart home standards and interoperability will become increasingly important as the number of smart devices and systems continue to grow. Standardization and interoperability will ensure that different devices can communicate and work together seamlessly, creating a more cohesive and integrated smart home ecosystem.

Step 9: Integration with Smart Cities

Smart homes will also become more integrated with smart cities, with homes and buildings playing a key role in creating sustainable, efficient, and connected urban environments. Smart homes will be able to communicate with other smart devices and systems in the city, providing data and insights that can be used to optimize energy usage, transportation, and other city services.

Step 10: Personalized Automation

Personalized automation will become more prevalent in smart homes, with devices and systems learning our preferences and habits and adapting to our needs in real-time. With personalized automation, our homes will become even more intuitive and responsive, anticipating our needs and taking action before we even ask.

By staying up to date on these future developments, we can prepare ourselves for the exciting possibilities and challenges that lie ahead. As smart homes become more advanced and interconnected, they will continue to transform the way we live and interact with our homes, creating a more connected, efficient, and sustainable world.

Final Words

The world of smart homes is constantly evolving and providing

innovative solutions to make our lives easier, more convenient, and

more efficient. With the right devices and technologies, a smart home

can help us save time, money, and energy while improving our quality

of life.

Smart homes have the potential to be particularly useful in areas where electricity is unreliable or not readily available, such as in Lebanon, where private generators are often used. With smart devices that can be powered by batteries or solar energy, a smart home can provide a reliable and sustainable source of power.

In addition, smart homes can also be a valuable tool for those with chronic pain or fatigue, providing automation and personalized settings that can help alleviate some of the challenges of daily life. For

introverts, smart home technology can provide a way to manage daily

interactions with ease, such as speaking to delivery people through a

smart home assistant rather than having to talk on the phone.

As we have explored in this guide, there are many different types of

smart devices and technologies available, and choosing the right ones

for your home can make all the difference. By setting up your smart home properly, creating smart routines, prioritizing security and privacy, and staying up to date on the latest developments in smart home technology, you can enjoy all the benefits that a smart home has to offer.

In the end, a smart home is about making life easier and more enjoyable. With the right tools and strategies, you can create a cost-effective, efficient, and personalized smart home that meets your needs and helps you achieve your goals. So, let's embrace the world of

smart homes and make our lives smarter, simpler, and more connected

than ever before.

www.ingramcontent.com/pod-product-compliance
Lightning Source LLC
Chambersburg PA
CBHW070252230526
45470CB00002B/577